Child Pr[o]
the Hug[uenots]

finished 29th May 2020 (handwritten)

Excerpts and accounts of the prophetic move
of the Spirit in France 1688-1702 from the
French book
"The Sacred Theatre of the Cevennes"

Commissioned by Kathie Walters
by Francois Maximileon Mission
Translated by Claire Uyttebrouck

ISBN:1-888081-33-3
978-1-888081-33-6

Published by

Good News Fellowship Ministries
220 Sleepy Creek Rd
Macon, GA 31210

format by Lisa Walters Buck
info@lisawbuckdesign.com
www.lisawbuckdesign.com

Table of Contents

Introduction

First published in London in 1707, this book is a collection of testimonies about the "Small Prophets of the Cévennes," these young boys and girls, sometimes infants, who called the Protestant people to repentance and later on to resistance.

This book highlights a little known prophetic movement which took place between 1688 and 1702 in the South of France (Drôme, Vivarais, Cévennes and Bas Languedoc).

These witnesses, who were also fighters, affirm their unwavering convictions and tell how they became prophetic, and how their prophetic gift led them to take arms to fight for their freedom of conscience. Many of them went into exile in England, Switzerland, Holland and Germany.

Children Caught Up in the Spirit

Suddenly, at the end of the 17th century, in the area of the Cévennes, babies stood up in their cribs and called people to repent. Young children of three and five, teenagers of twelve, fifteen, and seventeen rolled around on the floor and prophesied, announcing the deliverance of the people of Israel (meaning the Protestants (Huguenots) and the destruction of Babylon.

When caught up in the Spirit, the children spoke the language of their Bible, French, although their mother tongue is the local Patois. They could neither read nor write. Children and adults alike didn't remember what they said when they came back or they only remembered very little. Everything started in the Dauphiné with a shepherdess, in 1688. Isabeau Vincent, fifteen years old, spoke with her eyes closed, commented on the Bible and called sinners to repent. People listened to her. She was arrested, thrown in jail, but she kept preaching.

In 1689, a young peasant boy called Gabriel Astier prophesied and drew crowds to himself. Then hundreds of children, sometimes only three or four years old, "fell in a state of ecstasy". Nine month old babies prophesied in their crib. Some children prophets were denounced by their parents to the authorities, arrested and thrown in jail. Some of them escaped, then were adopted by the Camisard families.

Louis XIV revoked the Edict of Nantes in 1685, and after that, the Protestant faith was forbidden. Pastors were deported out of France. Massive forced conversions to Catholicism began. Persecutions were fierce and deadly, but the prophetic movement spread. In the beginning it was entirely peaceful, the "small prophets" (small because of their young age and size) called the people to reconcile, to repent, and to a completely break off from the Catholic Church. Then, in a second stage, prophecy became warlike.

Mazel, a simple peasant from the Cévennes, was the first one to call people to "holy war" and to avenge against the torturing clergy. They had the right to have people hanged, beaten to death or imprisoned for life. It was the Holy Spirit who told Mazel to take arms, and it's by His revelation that the Camisards heard about traitors among them, avoided ambushes, discover conspiracies, and hit their enemies. All their decisions were inspired by the Spirit. Thanks to this, a group of simple peasants regularly defeated a trained army.

4

Prophetic Troops

The leaders among them were the most prophetic men, and at least half of the troops had the gift of prophecy. They didn't need watchmen, for it was the Spirit who warned them when there was danger. Some fighters had the gift of prayer and exhortation, others received warnings for the Church, and still others received specific warnings for specific situations. The more they listened and obeyed, the more victorious they were. All of them had an incredible zeal for God's glory and totally yielded to His will, whether in life or in death.

Pastors

At the time, the Catholic authorities ignored the pastors. They thought they where the same as priests. They thought that if the Pastor is no longer there to take care of the flock, the sheep will waste away and scatter.

One only had to observe what a pastor truly was in any given village to see the difference with a priest. The big difference was that Protestants read their Bible every day. The pastor's role was quite clear: he's the most instructed brother and helped the others to better understand the difficult passages of Scriptures. He was the guide who acknowledged the full autonomy of his brothers' faith and helped them grow into their full potential. Instead of being God's spokesperson like a priest, he was the wise man -- the expert of the community who encouraged the others.

Prophets said that when they were taken up in the Spirit, it was something wonderful and divine. They started shivering and feeling weak -- as if feverish. They would yawn several times and then fall down and close their eyes. They stayed down for a while then they suddenly woke up and started prophesying. They said they saw the open Heaven, angels, paradise, and hell. Prophets prophesied not only during assemblies, but also in the countryside or in their houses. Small assemblies gathered, 400 to 500 people, major ones 3,000 to 4,000. For several years, they gathered in the woods, in caves, and in other isolated places. They all preached repentance, this is a theme found in all testimonies. The Bible was quoted in French by people who cannot read or write French, and who hardly knew French.

When Isabeau, the fifteen year old girl, was in prison, she prophesied more than ever. She told her torturers that they may kill her, because God will raise up many child prophets who will tell even greater things than she does.

Responsible for Self & Child Prophets

Each person, by reading the Bible, becomes his own priest. The Gospel can be spread without clergy, without religious authorities, without hierarchy. Pastors having been deported, the lay people filled in by simply devoting more time than others to the needs of the church.

Every person is responsible for himself and co-responsible for the community, irrespective of institutions, which is a deeply democratic and indirectly revolutionary concept.

Because "churches" had collapsed due to persecutions, there were no more pastors and no more fundamental freedoms. So little groups popped up and tried to make up for this institutional void.

In an assembly, a witness saw a young girl who could hardly read. She said she couldn't preach, but the Spirit preached through her. She started praying and her prayer was so beautiful he thought he was seeing an angel. Then she sang a Psalm and she sounded like an angel. She then started preaching and what she said was so beautiful, so zealous, and so full of wisdom that it was obvious it was divine. She quoted the Old Testament and the New Testament as if she knew the whole Bible by heart. She illustrated passages with such accuracy that everyone was dumbfounded. She lamented on the state of the church and said, "It's due to our sins." Then she comforted the people in an incredibly gentle way and promised mercy, peace, blessings, fulfillment, and eternal joy to all those who received the Lord.

Another witness mentions a girl from Languedoc, who received revelations. When she was in the Spirit, she was capable of saying things about this witness that she could not have known naturally. An angel "stirs her organs and gets her to say what the Spirit orders."

Jean Vernet testified in 1707 that the first people he saw in the Spirit were his mother, his brother, two of his sisters, and a cousin. His mother, ignorant of only the French language, spoke it when she was in the Spirit. While visiting friends, he saw a fourteen month old baby prophesying in French, although this child had never said a word before. The baby spoke with a loud voice and called people to repentance. There were about twenty people in the room and everyone was cut to the heart and wept. He also heard about an infant, not yet weaned, who prophesied in the same way. It often happened that these small prophets warned the assembly that they needed to break up because soldiers were coming. When they didn't heed that word immediately, they were caught, thrown in prison or sent to the galleys.

Thousands of children prophesied and the Catholic authorities claimed they were impostors and they were taught what they were saying. These children were tortured, flogged, the soles of their feet where burned, but they kept prophesying. They were brought to a Medical School to be examined, and from time to time they were seized by the Spirit and began to prophesy. It is obvious that those children were totally illiterate and that their discourse didn't match their age or their level of instruction, as they could quote the Bible and say things they obviously had never learned. They ended up being called fanatics.

A Man Named Mazel

As prophets filled the jails, the court gave the order to stop imprisoning, and to simply slaughter those who still gathered together. Only then did the people start to take arms to defend themselves, and only after a man named Mazel received the order from the Holy Spirit to do so.

Thousands of women didn't stop prophesying and singing hymns, although they were being hanged by the hundreds. Several witnesses mentioned slaughtered brothers who "had the honor to suffer martyrdom." Everytime those who were being mistreated, imprisoned, and tortured -- seem full of joy, sang hymns, and prayed to God continually.

Two witnesses told two different stories, where people in the Spirit said that God would destroy Babylon (the Catholic church) and restore His Church. These people couldn't read and yet they spoke French well when in the Spirit.

One witness said he went to a place where he was told an assembly would be taking place, but when he got there with a few friends, the place was empty. When they prayed to find the meetings and a bright light appeared in the sky, like a big star, and led them to where the assembly was, about half a mile away. Another witness said that it was the light in the sky that enabled him to find his way back to his regiment of Camisards.

Among the troop of Camisards, Mazel fell into a state of ecstasy and announced the imminent death of one of the brothers during combat. Once he "woke up," he identifies the brother about to die and advised him to get ready. This brother accepted the news with resignation, and a few weeks later he was mortally wounded by a bullet.

In fact, all the brothers in the troop who were called to die, either during combat or because they would be executed, were warned in advance by the Spirit, so that they could say their goodbyes to their family and prepare to glorify God in their death as they had during their lifetime. The Spirit was by their side until their last breath, which for them, was simply a passage from one life to the next.

But most of the time, the Camisards received words of knowledge telling them they have nothing to fear in combat, and they would all come back with incredible stories of bullets being caught between their shirt and their skin without having wounded them. As a result, bullets were as inconsequential as rain to them, and young boys of twelve fought the "lions" with their sling, just like David with Goliath. They all lived in the most serious purity and discipline, and as the Spirit forbade them to take any spoil, they sometimes burned true treasures.

In a home, a witness saw a six year old boy fall in the Spirit and prophesy that a part of the great Babylon would be destroyed. Another boy of eight prophesied that the Protestant faith would be re-established in France. In the assemblies, some people spoke what sounded like a foreign language, and then someone else "interpreted."

A witness said that a young girl of eighteen prophesied to him that he would be arrested the next day, but he that didn't have to fear because he would be released that same day. That's exactly what happened.

Sometimes, those in the Spirit saw armies of angels. At times these angels fought against armies of demons in the sky. It was prophesied on several occasions that God would have fires or lights fall from the sky during the night to blind the eyes of the enemies or to guide His people, and that's what happened.

A young girl fell in the Spirit and prophesied that there would be many ordeals in the land, but a "new world" would arise. She interceded so that the country will not be struck by lightning, and started to weep tears of blood. Some people who knew her well said that it was not the first time they saw her shed tears of blood.

"Beginning on August 24, 1572 and lasting for nearly two months afterward, tens of thousands of men, women and children were slaughtered across France...in a religious war."

source: http://www.todayifoundout.com/index.php/2014/03/
st-bartholomews-day-massacre/

Account of Jean Cavalier, Head of the Camisards

Jean said that he joined an assembly gathering in a barn out of sheer curiosity, for the things of God didn't interest him. When he got there, a little boy was shaking in the Spirit on the floor and he inwardly laughed at him. The little boy then said that there were people in the assembly who only came out of curiosity, with a mocking spirit, and he portrayed Jean so accurately that he was ashamed and headed towards the door to leave. At that moment a second young boy fell in the Spirit, right in front of the door, making it impossible for Jean to leave. The boy talked about a malicious person trying to leave. Jean was all the more uncomfortable, until he heard another child preach in such a way that it cut him to the heart and he started to pray. All fear left Jean and he asked God to get to know His will. God's zeal fell on him. The child preached with such conviction that the whole assembly was in tears. He preached for about two hours and nobody missed a minute of it. Everyone knew that the child could not read, didn't know any French (although he taught in French), and didn't have the education to say what he said.

Jean was deeply converted by this child's words and wept profusely when he was confronted with his sins. Then he felt like a hammer hit his chest and fire spread through his veins and into his whole body. He lost balance and fell down. The heat intensified, the fire increased, and he shook uncontrollably. He remembered his sexual immorality and was convicted of sin like never before. Meanwhile, the child kept preaching and said that he was blessed to have been called by God to be filled up with His grace, and that he needed to thank Him with a grateful heart. As he grumbled, the child went on to say that God's will was to hold him for a while before receiving spiritual gifts, and in the meantime he needed to pray unceasingly.

Jean went back home totally transformed, still in tears and sometimes losing balance as if he was drunk. He stayed in that state for nine months. God's hand often touched him but his tongue is still tied. However, God's grace comforted him as he obeyed the Spirit who prompted him to pray. Sin no longer tempted him, nor was he drawn to Cathelicism.

After nine months of tears and shaking without words, Jean fell into an exceptional state of ecstasy and God opened his mouth. For three days he was in the Spirit and didn't eat, drink, or sleep. He only preached and urged people to repent, and all the people who saw him were convinced that it was the Spirit speaking through him.

He then decided to join the Camisards, peasant fighters, prompted by the Holy Spirit to fight the King's army which slaughtered Protestant men, women and children without mercy. One day he was sitting down at table with his comrades in arms and received a word of knowledge that there was a Judas among them who intended to poison everyone. Another brother received a word that the traitor intended to poison the water of the cistern. A third person received the revelation that the traitor still has the poison on him and would try to hide it or throw it away, but he will be unmasked and exposed...

...And indeed, the traitor was confronted by someone who learned from the Spirit exactly where the poison was hidden, and went to get it. But they decided to let him live and release him. The traitor then denounced everyone to the authorities and Jean is made prisoner with about 60 of his comrades.

Painting of Jean Cavalier

source: https://commons.wikimedia.org/wiki/File:Jean_
Cavalier_chef_camisard.jpg

Jean is Made Prisoner

Jean travelled on a ship and found himself in the midst of a great storm. One of the prisoners received a word saying that within four hours they would arrive safely, and that's what happened.

In the jail where they were imprisoned, they saw the traitor again. He had a dream where he falls into a heap of garbage and choked to death. A few days later he became ill and literally vomited garbage and died.

Some time later, Jean was released from prison although he had been sentenced to life in prison. He went back home. During the Sunday worship, the head of the assembly, brother Clary, was seized by the Spirit and learned that there were two traitors in the group who only came to spy, but they would be unmasked. Indeed, the Spirit led him to the two traitors, who immediately repented and said it was out of poverty that they were working for the enemy. Clary has them bound, but the Spirit told him people were grumbling because they believe that if the traitors repented so quickly, it is because Clary was their accomplice.

The Holy Spirit then addresses the assembly through Clary and convicted them of their lack of faith. The Spirit says that in order to show them His power, He's going to put Clary on a stake to be burned but he would not be affected. The assembly pleaded to not burn him because they didn't believe that he was going to survive.

A stake was built and Clary positioned himself in the middle. Someone lit it and the flames were higher than his head. When the flames died down, Clary got out unharmed, without even the smell of smoke in his hair or clothes. Then the traitors were released.

Painting of a group of Huguenots in hiding:

source: https://en.wikipedia.org/wiki/Karl_Girardet

Calling Everyone to Repentance

Another witness told the story of a young girl, ten to twelve years old, who fell in the Spirit in the house of a gardener. When she started talking, she told everyone to keep quiet because in the garden there was a man who could betray them. The gardener went out and saw a surgeon, a known persecutor, collecting plants for a remedy. Once the surgeon was gone, the girl started to preach, calling everyone to repentance, which would bring a shower of blessings on all. However, if they kept sinning, the country will be hit by the most terrifying judgments from God. This girl spoke in French, although she had never studied it, and quoted many passages from Scriptures, although she couldn't read.

A few months later, the same witness saw people rushing to a house as he was walking down the street. He followed them and saw a girl who had just fallen in the Spirit. She said approximately the same thing as the former girl and finished up with a long and beautiful prayer.

A few days later, he went to visit a young girl, six or seven years old, accompanied by a priest. She was seized by the Spirit and started to preach. The priest couldn't believe his ears. When she "woke up," he tried to convince her to tell him who taught her those things, but she claimed she doesn't control anything she does or says, it wasn't her but something that "takes over". The priest realized that it was ridiculous to see any malice in this child, or in any child preaching or prophesying that way, but because of his position, he feels compelled to say it was by the power of the devil that those children spoke the way they do.

Another witness said that it was "the village half-wit" who preached best and had the most beautiful sermons. She could not speak four words of French and was normally very shy in public. The witness said: "This Balaam's donkey has a mouth filled with gold when the Spirit speaks through her." No speaker was listened to the way she was, and no audience was more captivated or moved. Her eloquence flow was a pure wonder. This woman could control when she fell in the Spirit. When people came to visit her and hear her preach, she just needed to say a short prayer and the Spirit came to "take over", and the Holy Spirit preached and prophesied through her.

Another witness told the story of a young girl of eight or nine who regularly fell in the Spirit. At those times, she only breathed through sighs, her breast was heaving and all her body was shaking.

Other Christian Historical Books by David & Kathie Walters

The Celtic Dove

This book is about St. Columba of Iona, an island of the coast of Scotland. Columba had a monastery there where he taught and trained hundreds of young men to preach the Gospel, heal the sick, raise the dead. This book is filled with eyewitness accounts of Columba's amazing prophetic gift, the miracles, and many angelic visitations. It was first compiled by St. Adamnan around 692-A.D. – 697 A.D..

Celtic Flames

This book is about the amazing lives of seven great saints:

Brendan of Clonfert 448 A.D.-581 A.D.

Cuthbert of Landisfarne 634 A.D.– 687 A.D.

Columba of Iona. 521 A.D.- 597 A.D.

Brigid First Abbess of Kildare 453 A.D. – 524 A.D.

Patrick The Celtic Lion 389 A.D.-471 A.D.

Comgall Abbot of Bangor 516 A.D.-601 A.D.

Kieran, First Bishop of Saiger 352-A.D.-540 A.D.

Bangor Light Of The World

Much of our present day 24 hour IHOP have been patterned on this history of Bangor. This account is a brief history of the Bangor Monastery. The monastery had around 250 years of non stop prayer and praise. The High Choir was famous all over the world. Many people were sent out from there to take the Gospel into Europe How did it start? Why did it stop? What happened in between?

Children Aflame With The Spirit

Amazing little known accounts from the journals of John Wesley. 1703-1791 A.D. Wesleyan Revivals with children from 1730-1780, including modern day Revivals with children for more than 40 years in the ministry of David Walters.

What Happened To Evan Roberts And The 1904 Welsh Revival?

Like a tree shaken by a mighty storm, Wales was moved by the power of God until almost every home in the nation felt its impact! So great was the fear of God, conviction gripped the people and in some communities crime disappeared. God used a young 26 year old Bible student, Evan Roberts. Read what happened and how this most amazing move of God which covered Wales began to wane and change. Why did the revival go? What happened to Evan Roberts? Why did he start having nervous breakdowns? We need to know these things and not make the same mistakes in the future.

Bright And Shining Revival

An account of the Hebrides Revival 1948-1952. The Hebrides Islands are a small group of islands off the west coast of Scotland. In 1948-1952 God poured out His Spirit in response to a handful of praying men and women. It doesn't take multitudes to move the hand of God but those who are determined to push through the crowd and touch the hem of his garment. Whole towns were saved as the presence of God chased people Kathie Walters visited the islands and the people several times to obtain first hand knowledge of the revival.

The Irish Slaves In America

Most people in America are ignorant of the huge indignity and cruel treatment of the Irish Catholics. Why is it so hidden? Why isn't it taught in schools as many Americans are from these very immigrant people who were forced to come to the U.S. as slaves and many died in the process? Over 800,000 men, women and children, were sold as slaves.

Teaching CD's by Kathie Walters

<u>Getting Free and Living in the Supernatural</u>

<u>In Depth for Seers and Prophets</u>

<u>Spiritual Strategies</u>

<u>The Almond Tree</u>

<u>The Fanatic in the Attic</u>

<u>Faith and Angels</u>

<u>Revival Accounts and Getting your Family Saved</u>

Other Books by Kathie Walters

Living in the supernatural

The Spirit of False Judgment

The Visitation

Parenting By the spirit

Angels Watching Over You

The Bright and Shining Revival

Seer List

Elitism & The False Shepherding Spirit

Health Related Mindsets

Contact:

Kathie ministers in churches, conferences, and women's conferences. She believes that the realm of the Spirit, the supernatural realm, the angels, miracles etc. are meant to be a normal part of the life of every Christian. The religious spirit prevents Gods people from receiving their inheritance.

For further information on Kathie or David Walters ministry visit:

Website: http://www.KathieWaltersMinistry.com

E-mail: kathiewalters@mindspring.com

or write or call:

Good News Ministries

(478) 757-8071

220 Sleepy Creek Rd.

Macon GA 31210

Tour of Ireland & Scotland with Kathie Walters

Come to Ireland and Scotland on a 14-Day Celtic Heritage Tour with Kathie Walters!

- Re-dig the spiritual wells of this beautiful country
- Pray on the Hill of Slane where St. Patrick lit his Pascal fire and defied the High King.
- See the place where St. Patrick first landed to bring the Gospel to Ireland by God through the Angel of Ireland, Victor.
- See the green hills and dales of Ireland - a picture you will never forget.
- Visit the ancient places of worship that will help enable you to grasp hold of your godly inheritance.

Then on to Scotland

    • Tour the beautiful highlands of Scotland.

    • Visit the island of Iona, where St. Columba built his monastery. See beautiful Loch Ness and Loch Lomond and visit Edinburgh.

Printed by Amazon Italia Logistica S.r.l.
Torrazza Piemonte (TO), Italy

13643691R00025